THE LOST ART OF

TOWEL ORIGAMI

Alison Jenkins

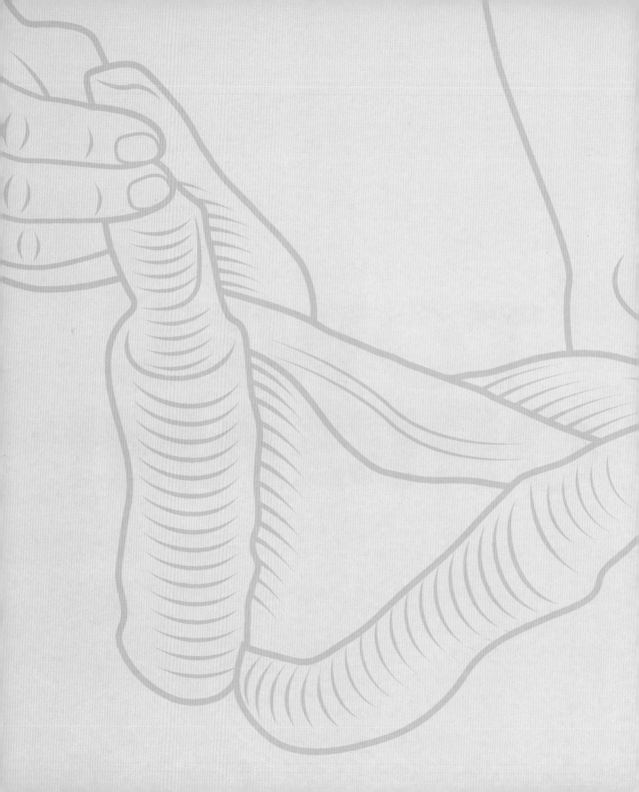

THE LOST ART OF
TOWEL ORIGAMI

Alison Jenkins

Bath time will NEVER be the same AGAIN!

**Andrews McMeel
Publishing**

Kansas City

ANDREWS McMEEL PUBLISHING,LLC,
an Andrews McMeel Universal company,
4520 Main Street,
Kansas City, Missouri 64111.

ISBN-13: 978-0-7407-5563-7
ISBN-10: 0-7407-5563-3

This book was conceived,
designed, and produced by:
THE IVY PRESS LIMITED
The Old Candlemakers, West Street,
Lewes, East Sussex, BN7 2NZ, UK.

Creative Director Peter Bridgewater
Publisher Sophie Collins
Editorial Director Jason Hook
Senior Project Editor Hazel Songhurst
Art Director Karl Shanahan
Designer Joanna Clinch
Photographer Simon Punter

Originated and printed in Thailand.

06 07 CTP 08 09 10 9 8 7 6 5 4

Introduction

TOWEL ORIGAMI is one of the more intriguing arts once practiced by our forebears. Its exact origins are unknown but they have been the subject of much speculation. It has been said that while Queen Cleopatra bathed in milk—which could be for hours at a time—her servants kept her entertained by fashioning cloths into amusing shapes. Another theory has its roots in the frivolous 1920s, when passengers on cruises filled the empty hours in between sipping cocktails by modeling their towels.

Since the real truth is a mystery, you can pick whichever explanation you like the most. What is important to us today is that this unique ancient craft has been rediscovered! Everywhere, happy vacationers are delighted to discover a towel in the shape of an elephant or a swan on their pillow when they return from a day at the beach. (A fun change from the usual chocolate!)

Unlike towel origami, the roots of paper origami can be traced back to the ancient Japanese tradition of presenting an intricately folded paper certificate with a precious gift. By the late 19th century, this functional craft of paper folding had become a popular decorative art form.

There is clearly a huge difference between creating towel origami and the paper variety: You make paper origami models from neat, crisp, easy-to-fold squares, whereas towel origami models are folded from floppy, fluffy, soft rectangles in a variety of thicknesses and sizes.

The success or failure of traditional origami relies on accuracy and the need for straight, crisp creases in your material—but let's face it, towels just don't respond in the same way as paper. This permits a certain amount of artistic license in this far less disciplined, much more lighthearted form of origami.

Unlike paper origami, the lost art of towel origami leans heavily toward a range of "molding" techniques combined with simple, basic folding methods. All the models featured in this book have been created using these same methods, so you should be able to replicate them easily.

Rest assured that the newly rediscovered art of towel origami requires no special skills, equipment, or even patience. Results are achieved in minutes and it's fun to do! A serious sense of humor is all that's required.

Begin by mastering the basic techniques on the pages that follow, then move on to the individual projects. Each model has been awarded a difficulty rating, and it is recommended that you begin with an "easy" project and tackle a "moderate" or "difficult" one when you feel more confident.

1 easy

2 moderate

3 difficult

Whether you choose to fold towels for your own enjoyment or for the entertainment of your family or house guests, take pleasure in your newfound folding skills. Bath time will never, ever be the same again!

Basic Folds and Techniques

Due to the soft, fluffy nature of bath towels, you will understand that the typical crisp folds that are the result of traditional paper origami cannot be re-created exactly. However, most of the very basic traditional folding techniques are employed, alongside more unusual methods, to produce very interesting creations. There is a certain amount of "molding" involved and a fair smattering of slightly more forceful manipulation, too! Here are a few techniques to master before you begin the projects.

Basic Symbols

----- Dotted lines represent a fold line: either a fold that is made and left creased, or one that is made creased then opened out flat again to indicate the center or a division of the towel's length or width.

This symbol means that you must turn the whole shape over, keeping all previous folds or shaping intact. If necessary, slip one hand under the shape and place the other hand on top, then quickly flip it over.

⟶ Arrows indicate the direction in which the fabric of the towel should be folded, rolled, tucked, or drawn out.

Basic Folds

All the shapes featured in this book begin with a towel that is laid out on a flat surface like the floor or a bed. Make sure that you follow the instructions carefully, and always begin exactly as instructed with the towel laid out horizontally or vertically, as this will affect the final shape of your creation.

Towel Laid Horizontally

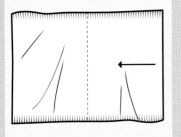

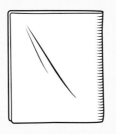

Folding in half widthways
With the towel laid out horizontally, take the furthest right-hand edge

and bring it over to meet the left-hand edge. Now run the palm of your hand along the fold to make a crease.

This can be done the opposite way if the instructions direct.

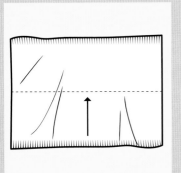

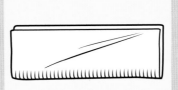

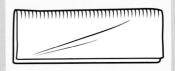

Folding in half lengthways
With the towel laid out horizontally, take the lower edge and bring it

upward to meet the upper edge. Now run the palm of your hand along the fold to make a crease.

This can be done the opposite way if the instructions direct.

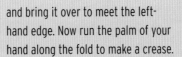

Towel Laid Vertically

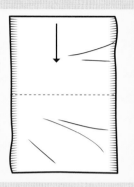  

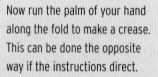

Folding in half widthways

With the towel laid out vertically, take the uppermost edge and bring it down to meet the lower edge.

Now run the palm of your hand along the fold to make a crease. This can be done the opposite way if the instructions direct.

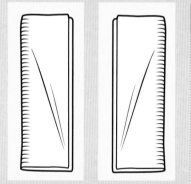

Folding in half lengthways

Take the left-hand edge and bring it over to meet the right-hand edge. Now run the palm of your hand

along the fold to make a crease. This can be done the opposite way if the instructions direct.

NOTE

Use the folding and creasing method to divide the towel into thirds, quarters, or smaller divisions. Fold the towel as required, press the folds to crease, then either use the shape as directed or open up and use the crease lines as markers for further folds.

Rolling and Stretching

Using towels to make models allows for rolling and stretching, whereas traditional origami paper does not. Follow these simple steps to achieve a perfect elephant trunk, a swan neck, or a monkey or dog body. Some of these techniques take a little while to master, and sometimes a certain amount of force is needed to encourage the model to take the correct shape.

Basic roll

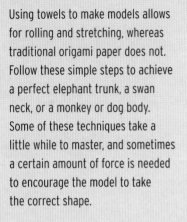

1 Fold and crease the towel to indicate the center line, then open it out flat again.

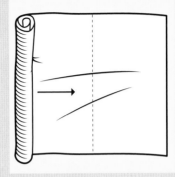

2 Beginning at one short edge, roll the towel tightly toward the center crease line.

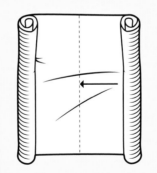

3 Roll up the other half of the towel in the same way, toward the center line.

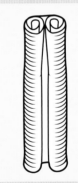

4 The finished shape: Two tight rolls lying parallel to each other.

11

Monkey body

This may take a few attempts to get right, and it involves some pulling and heaving!

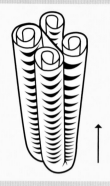

1 Begin with the basic rolled shape (see p. 11).

2 Fold the rolled shape in half with the rolls facing upward.

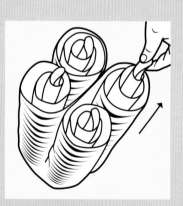

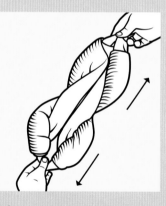

3 Now, this is the difficult part! Pull out the corner of the towel from the center of each roll.

4 Try to hold two corners in one hand and two in the other. Pull the corners away from each other.

5 The folded towel will stretch out to form two legs and two arms. Now manipulate the shape to style it.

Diagonal roll

This fold or roll forms the perfect elephant trunk and swan neck, and is customized a little to form the dog head (see p. 62).

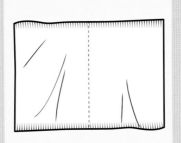

1 Begin with a towel placed horizontally with the center line indicated as shown.

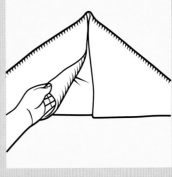

2 Bring the top two corners down to meet the center line, then press the folds flat.

TOP TIP

This type of rolled shape can easily come unrolled, so it sometimes helps to secure the shape using a safety pin that can easily be disguised with a pair of sunglasses.

3 Roll along each diagonal edge toward the center line.

4 Hold one roll in each hand and twist toward the center tightly. The pointed part will curl into shape.

13

Pointed Flaps and Tucks

These simple folds result in pointed flaps that can be folded in two directions, and the tuck method allows a right-angled corner to be softened to create a slightly more rounded silhouette.

The first method is employed for the windmill and the angel fish, while the second is useful for molding the heart, lips, and ladybug.

Pointed flaps

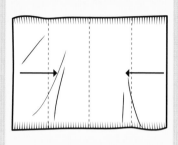

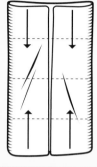

1 Fold a towel in half widthways. Crease the shape into quarters vertically then open out. Fold right and left sides to meet at the center.

2 Crease the shape to divide it into quarters horizontally then open out. Bring the top and lower edge to meet in the center.

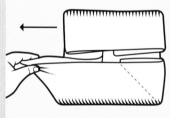

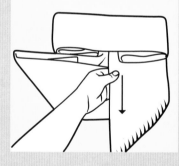

3 Press the shape flat with your palms, then reach inside the lower left-hand side of the shape to find the corner.

4 Pull the corner outward and left into a triangular pointed flap, which can be folded flat. Trace a line with your fingertip as shown by the dotted line.

5 Take the lower right-hand edge and fold it back along the indicated crease line. This makes it easier to bring out the point and fold it downward.

14

Tucks

1 Fold a towel in half horizontally then fold the corner as shown. Press the fold flat with your hand.

2 Keeping your left hand lightly on the folded part, pick up the top layer only of the towel and pull it out from under the folded corner.

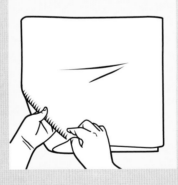

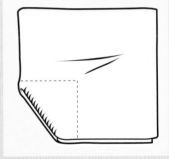

3 Your left hand will now slip inside the shape and the top layer will fall on top.

4 The result is that the corner is now tucked inside the shape to make a more rounded silhouette.

Happy Birthday

We've called this classic model a birthday cake, but it would be just as suitable as a wedding gift or a thoughtful housewarming token. Simple white towels are set off with striking red satin ribbons, but a similarly delightful effect can be achieved by using pastel or even chocolate-brown towels, with lace or tassel trimmings. If you give this towel arrangement as a gift, wrap it up in a large square of clear cellophane so the layers keep their shape.

YOU WILL NEED

2 BATH SHEETS
2 BATH TOWELS
2 HAND TOWELS
RIBBON TRIM
1 FACE CLOTH

easy

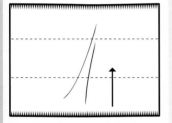

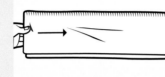

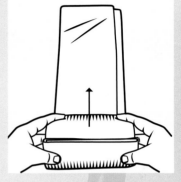

1 Lay one bath sheet out flat horizontally as shown and fold into thirds, folding the lower edge upward first so a fold, not an edge, lies across the top. If the towel is very wide, fold it into quarters.

2 Roll up the folded strip tightly from one end. Now fold the second bath sheet in the same way as the first.

3 Pln the end of the second towel to the edge of the first and roll it tightly around the first roll.

As an extra treat, decorate the top of each layer with a row of colorful foil-wrapped chocolates—these won't last till bath time, I can assure you!

TOP TIP

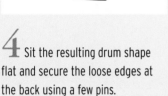

4 Sit the resulting drum shape flat and secure the loose edges at the back using a few pins.

5 Make the second layer of the cake in the same way, but this time using the two bath towels. Secure the edges at the back and set on top of the bottom layer.

6 Make the third layer in the same way using the two hand towels, and arrange it on top of the first and second layers.

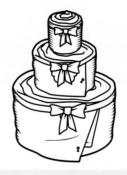

7 Wrap a length of colored satin ribbon around each layer of the "cake" and finish with pretty bows. You can use lace or other decorative trimmings or even cut-out paper bands, if you prefer.

8 Pick up a face cloth in the center and pinch it into points. Tuck the cloth into the top layer of the cake as a final decorative flourish.

Gift Basket

Surprise your unsuspecting house guests with a pretty basket brimming with bath-time goodies in their room. Choose scented soaps and attractively shaped bottles of bath foam or shampoo to match or coordinate with the color of your towels. You could even include a small bottle of champagne as a special treat for your guests to enjoy.

YOU WILL NEED	1 BATH TOWEL 1 FACE CLOTH SOAPS AND BATH PRODUCTS SAFETY PINS

moderate

 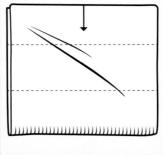

1 Lay the towel out flat vertically, then fold in half by bringing the lower edge upward to meet the top edge. Press the fold flat with the palm of your hand.

2 Divide the folded towel roughly into thirds, then fold along the crease lines, bringing the top edge downward first.

3 Divide the resulting shape roughly into thirds again and fold along the crease lines, pressing the folds firmly with the palm of your hand.

This basket is for decorative purposes only—it is quite robust and sturdy, but should not be carried around by the handle just in case the heavy bottles fall out!

TOP TIP

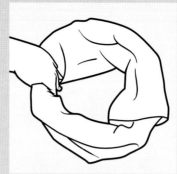

4 Open up the top layer on the left-hand side and tuck the right side into it to make a secure loop. Fix the edge in place using a safety pin.

5 Open up the loop, place your hand inside one of the folds in the middle, and push the towel down inside the loop to form a base for the basket shape.

6 Roll the corners of a face cloth to the center, then turn the shape over to the other side—this will form the handle. If your face cloth is quite soft, line the shape with a piece of tissue paper to give it rigidity.

7 Use safety pins to secure the pointed ends of the handle securely to each side of the top of the basket.

8 Fill the basket with pretty bath-time goodies, soaps, and perhaps another face cloth in a contrasting color as added decoration.

Fancy Fan

There are absolutely no fancy folding or molding techniques required to create this very simple yet classic model—it's all just plain, straight, parallel pleats. All you need to do is make sure that the pleats you make are the same width all the way along. Use towels that are the same color or try a contrast color for the smaller towel at the front.

YOU WILL NEED	1 BATH TOWEL 1 FACE CLOTH OR 1 GUEST TOWEL 2 ELASTIC BANDS 2 SAFETY PINS

easy

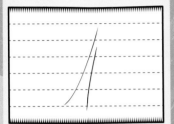

25

1 Lay the bath towel out flat horizontally. Fold and press regular parallel creases across the width about 4 in/10 cm apart. Use your fingers or a warm iron to make really sharp creases.

2 Pleat the towel up along the crease lines now and press flat along the folds with the palm of your hand.

3 Find the center of the pleated shape and secure at this point by winding an elastic band around it. Now fold the shape in half.

If you wash and starch your towels first, the folds of this model will look sharper. You could line the first folded shape with a sheet of tissue paper to help the folds keep their shape.

TOP TIP

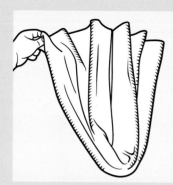

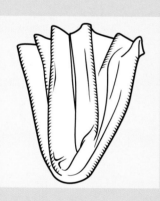

4 Use a safety pin to secure the top corners together, then allow the pleats to fall sideways away from the center.

5 Lay the fan shape flat on the bed or prop it up against the pillows at the bed head. Arrange the folds neatly and symmetrically.

6 Take a face cloth and make small pleats evenly across the whole length as shown. Find the center of the pleated shape as before and bind it with a small elastic band.

26

7 Fold the shape in half. Use a safety pin to secure the top edges together as before, then open out the smaller fan shape.

8 When you are satisfied with the fold arrangement of the large fan, place the smaller fan at the base.

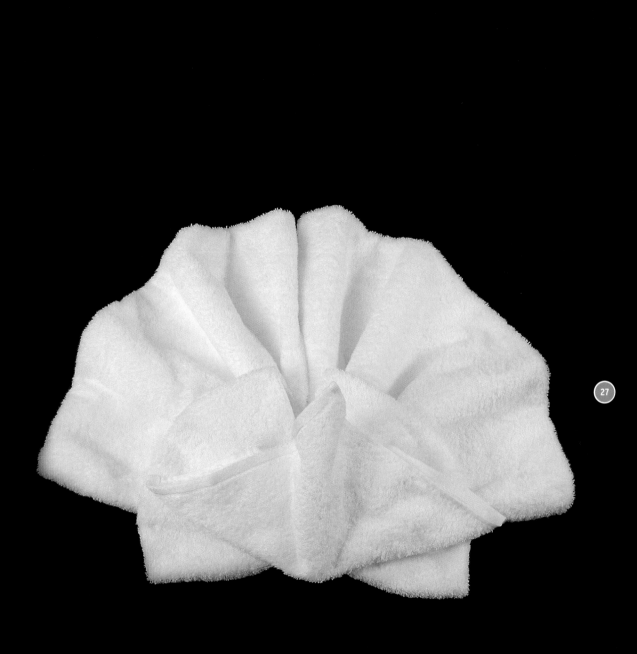

Spinning Windmill

You may remember making little paper windmills like this when you were a child—they actually spin in the wind when attached with a pin to a stick. Using the same simple folding principles, we made windmills from bath towels. Place the towel windmill on the corner of the bath tub or on a shelf and place some colored soap or a small sponge in the center.

YOU WILL NEED

1 BATH TOWEL OR HAND TOWEL

difficult

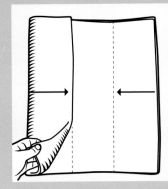

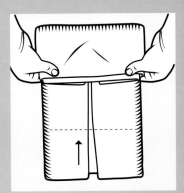

29

1 Lay the bath towel out flat horizontally as shown, then fold in half by bringing the left-hand edge across to meet the right-hand edge. Press the fold flat.

2 Fold the shape in half then in half again to divide the shape roughly into quarters. Open out again to indicate the divisions. Bring both sides in to meet at the center.

3 Fold and divide the shape roughly into quarters again but this time vertically, then bring the top and bottom edges toward the center.

You could make a small windmill using a square face cloth in a striped design to coordinate with the plain bath towel. Place it in the center of the larger shape.

TOP TIP

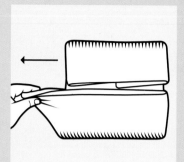

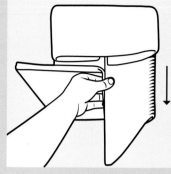

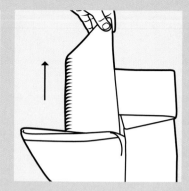

4 Find the left-hand corner that lies inside the lower fold and pull it outward, keeping the other folds in place as you do so.

5 Arrange the resulting triangular flap so it points to the left. Do the same with the right-hand corner, but this time arrange the flap so it points downward.

6 Pull out the upper left-hand corner in the same way and arrange it so the triangular flap points upward.

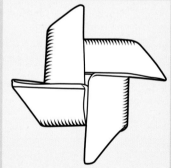

7 Do the same with the upper right-hand corner, and arrange the flap so it points to the right.

8 Your windmill is now complete. Rearrange the folds and edges where they meet and overlap at the center of the shape so they look neat and symmetrical.

Skyscraper

All you city slickers will love this one—
imagine a miniature Chrysler Building in
your bathroom! OK, it doesn't look
exactly the same, but it does give a
good impression and it is, after all,
made from bath towels! This model is
extremely useful when bathroom space
is at a premium because it stands up by
itself. Try balancing the shape on the
corner of the bathtub.

**YOU
WILL
NEED**

2 BATH TOWELS
1 BATH SHEET
SILVER-COLORED PAPER FOR
WINDOWS AND DETAILS
DOUBLE-SIDED TAPE

moderate

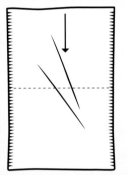

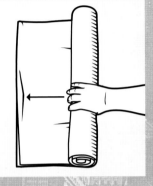

1 Lay one bath towel flat vertically, then fold in half, bringing the top edge down to meet the lower edge.

2 Roll up the towel tightly and evenly from the right-hand side toward the left, with the folded edge at the top.

3 Lay the bath sheet out flat horizontally as shown, then fold the towel roughly into thirds. Fold the left-hand edge first so there will be a fold, not an edge, lying at the right-hand side.

33

We made our skyscraper using white towels but the model would work just as well using gray or stone-colored ones.

TOP TIP

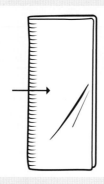

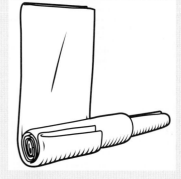

4 Lay the first rolled-up bath towel along the lower edge of the folded bath sheet. Then roll up both of them together, beginning at the lower edge.

5 Lay the second bath towel out flat vertically as shown, then fold in half by bringing the left-hand edge across to meet the right. Press the fold flat with the palm of your hand.

6 Place the rolled towel and bath sheet onto the folded bath towel as shown, then roll together. Pin the edges of the towels at the back of the shape so they do not unroll.

34

7 Stand the shape up on end. Now locate the towel edge at the center of the longest roll and pull gently outward to form a slim tapered point at the top.

8 Cut out the card shapes and windows (see templates pp. 78–79), then apply to the skyscraper. Use tabs of double-sided adhesive tape to hold the card shapes in position.

Tropical Palm

Need a reminder of the beach when it's cold and snowy outside? You can re-create a taste of the tropics in your bathroom any time of year—just use your bath towels! These amusing palm trees are simple enough to make that in a short time you could create a whole desert island full of palms gently swaying in the breeze.

YOU WILL NEED

1 BATH TOWEL
5 FACE CLOTHS
SAFETY PINS

moderate

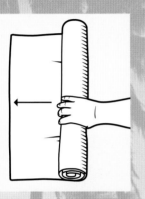

1 Lay the bath towel out flat horizontally and roll the towel up tightly and evenly across the width from the right-hand side to the left-hand side.

2 Grasp the roll firmly in one hand and find the corner of the towel inside the roll at the top. Pull the corner out of the roll to make the tapered tree trunk.

3 Now, tuck the lower ends of the trunk inside the lower rolled layers to make a thicker shape. Note: This shape will not stand up by itself and must be displayed flat.

Use brown towels and green face cloths for an authentic look. You could also place colored round soaps or candy at the top of the trunk to look like coconuts. If something is worth doing, then it's worth overdoing!

TOP TIP

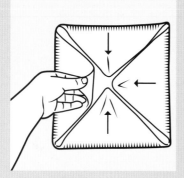

4 Now pick up a face cloth and bring all four corners together, making a pointed pyramid shape.

5 Hold three corners in one hand, then pull the fourth downward to form a leafy palm shape. You can pin the folds of the palm leaf with a safety pin if necessary.

38

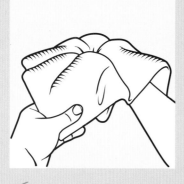

6 Do the same with the remaining face cloths to make four more palm leaf shapes. You can use more than five shapes if you fancy a really leafy palm tree.

7 Lay the tree on a flat surface and bend the shape slightly. Place the face cloth leaves at the top and arrange into a pleasing design.

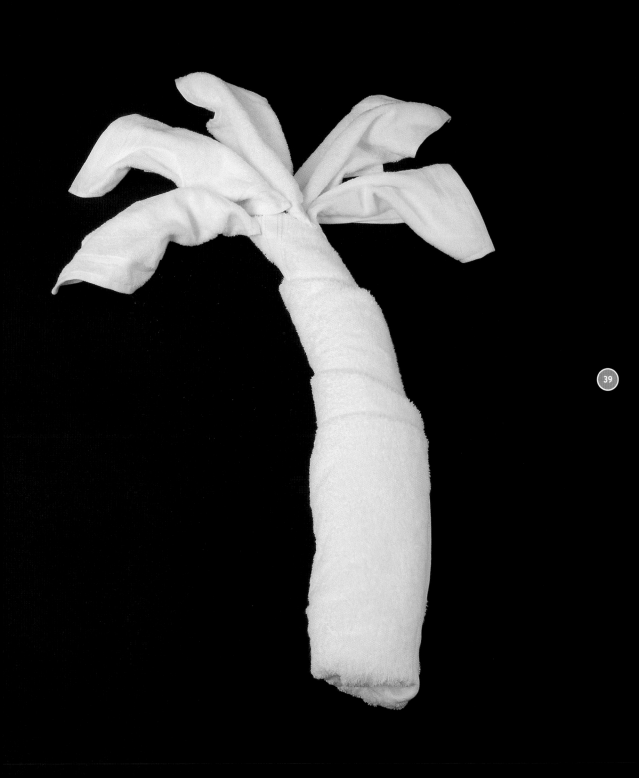

Lotus Flower

This is a traditional, lovely design reminiscent of the folded linen napkins you may find adorning your table at a special restaurant. It is just as effective when translated into towel form, and very attractive if the colors you use coordinate with the decor in your guest's bedroom or bathroom.

40

YOU WILL NEED	3 BATH TOWELS 1 FACE CLOTH SAFETY PINS (OPTIONAL)

difficult

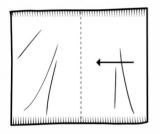

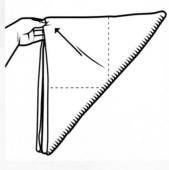

1 Lay one bath towel out flat horizontally, then fold in half widthways. Press the fold flat using the palm of your hand.

2 Fold the shape in half diagonally by bringing the lower right-hand corner up to meet the upper left-hand corner.

3 Place your index finger halfway along the diagonal edge and bring both the left- and the right-hand points toward the center. Press the shape firmly.

If you wash and starch your towels first, this model will stand up all by itself, but otherwise lay it flat or lean it against the pillows at the bed head. You may even find room for this model on a shelf at the end of the bathtub.

TOP TIP

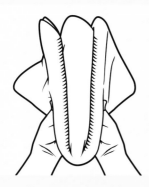

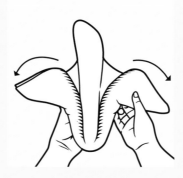

4 Keeping the shape flat, tuck the points at each side under the shape and pinch them together at the back.

5 Grasp the lower point in one hand, then peel the outer layers away from the central point to form a floral leafy shape.

6 Now peel the top layer of the central point outward and mold to make an even more pleasing and leafy shape.

42

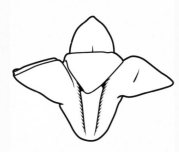

7 Squeeze the shape so that it keeps together (you could use a safety pin to help with this), then use the remaining towels to make two identical shapes.

8 Place the three shapes together to form the lotus flower, then fold a small face cloth in the same way and place at the base to disguise the point where the three larger shapes meet.

Kiss Me Lips

Move over, Mae West! Salvador Dali designed a sofa in the shape of luscious red lips so we've done the same—well, almost—using a luxurious bath towel. What a fantastic way to give someone you love a big kiss! We've used a standard-sized white bath towel, but you can make a really big kiss using a bright red bath sheet if you want to make a stunning statement!

YOU WILL NEED

1 BATH TOWEL

moderate

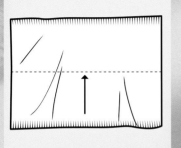

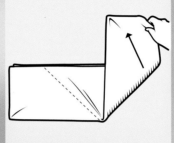

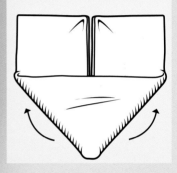

45

1 Lay the bath towel out flat horizontally, then fold in half by bringing the lower edge up to meet the upper edge. Press the fold flat using the palm of your hand.

2 Fold in half again widthways, press the fold flat to indicate the center line, then open out. Place your index finger at the base of the center line and bring the lower right-hand corner to lie along the center line.

3 Fold the left-hand side likewise, then slip your hand under the shape and place the other hand on top. Now flip the whole shape over to the other side, keeping the folds in place.

If you're not a purist, you can make your lips any color you like, bright pink, orange, purple . . . whatever takes your fancy.

TOP TIP

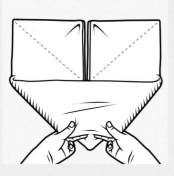

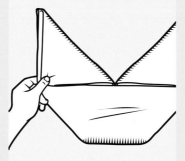

4 Fold and tuck the lower point underneath the shape to form the lower lip. Try a small fold first, then make it larger if necessary to achieve a pleasing shape.

5 Make a diagonal crease line from the center toward each of the top corners. Fold the right-hand shape along this line, then fold the left side likewise.

6 Now fold the top right-hand point downward to meet the center. This forms one half of the upper lip.

7 Now fold the top left-hand point to meet the center, then arrange the bath towel so that no tapes or edges are visible.

8 For a special finishing touch, plump up the completed lips by tucking some chocolates inside the folds of the upper and lower lips.

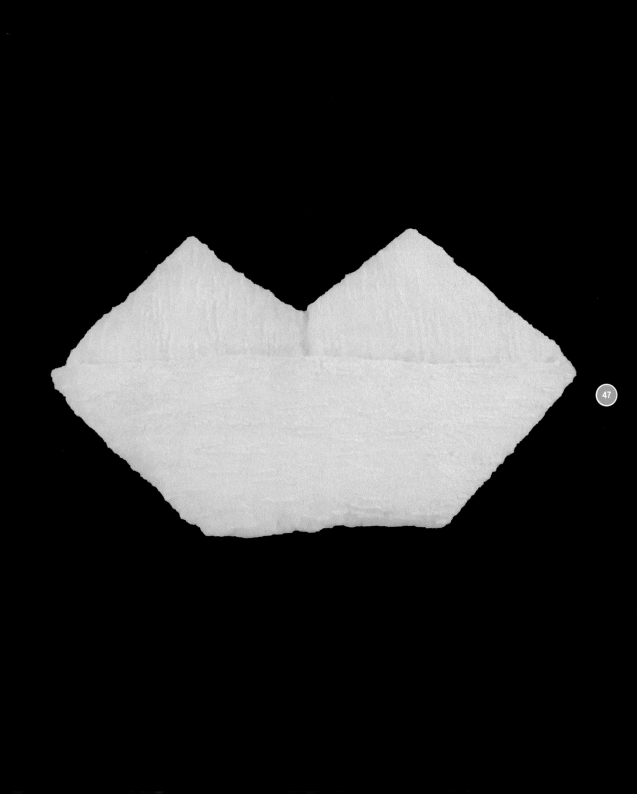

Love Heart

This one is an absolute must for all you true romantics out there—so simple to make and oh, so effective. Why not surprise your loved one on a special anniversary, a birthday, Valentine's Day, or on a perfectly ordinary day! The sentiment will be loud and clear—a great big heart that says "I love you!" Aaaah!

48

YOU WILL NEED

1 BATH TOWEL

easy

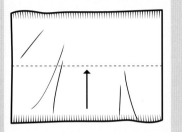
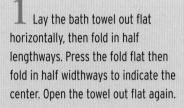
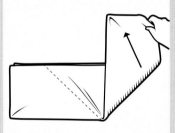
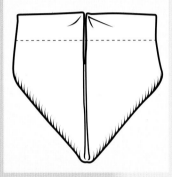

1 Lay the bath towel out flat horizontally, then fold in half lengthways. Press the fold flat then fold in half widthways to indicate the center. Open the towel out flat again.

2 Place your left index finger at the base of the center crease, then bring the lower right-hand edge toward the center. Press the diagonal fold flat.

3 Fold the left-hand side likewise. Crease the towel about 4 in/10 cm down from the top along both short edges. This measurement may vary according to the size of towel.

If your heart looks a bit flat, fold up two small matching face cloths and tuck them inside the heart shape to give it a plumper, more three-dimensional shape.

TOP TIP

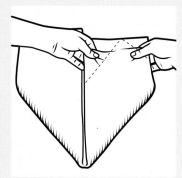

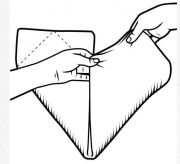

4 Tuck the short edges neatly behind the shape. Crease diagonally from the center of both short edges as shown.

5 Tuck the two points of the right-hand side either inside or just behind the shape to form the top lobes of the heart shape.

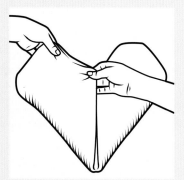

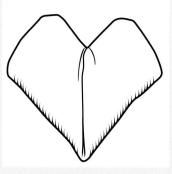

6 Fold and shape the left-hand side of the heart shape in exactly the same way so it matches the first.

7 Make sure that all the corners are tucked in neatly and that the shape has a softly rounded edge.

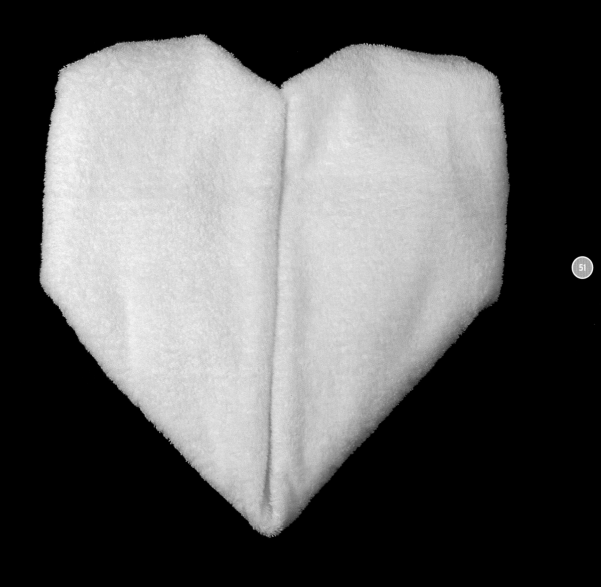

Ladybug, Ladybug!

Ladybug, ladybug, fly away home—but not before I've had a bath, thank you! This spotted bug requires just a few basic folding techniques together with a little "molding" to achieve a nice plump shape. The fluffy pipe-cleaner legs aren't absolutely necessary, but it does make this creature look more "bug-like," don't you think?

YOU WILL NEED	1 BATH TOWEL 3 FACE CLOTHS BLACK AND WHITE FELT 6 FLUFFY PIPE CLEANERS

moderate

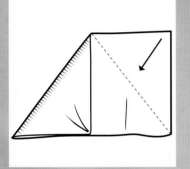 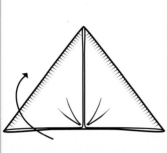 

1 Lay the bath towel out flat horizontally, fold in half to indicate the center line, then open out again. Bring both top corners down to meet at the center.

2 Press the diagonal folds flat using the palm of your hand. Slip one hand under the shape and lay the other flat on the top. Now flip the shape over, inverting the triangle at the same time.

3 Fold the top two corners downward to meet at the center, and tuck the lower point inside the shape. Press all the folds flat.

Red is the traditional color for a ladybug, but they do come in orange and yellow too, and some are even black with yellow or red spots. Just use your imagination.

TOP TIP

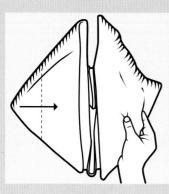

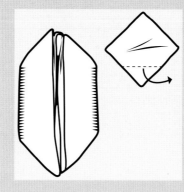

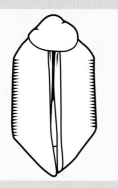

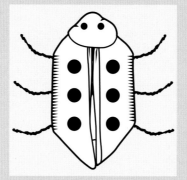

4 Tuck the corners on both sides inside the body shape. This makes a more rounded silhouette. Fold up two face cloths into quarters and tuck inside the wings to give the ladybug a plump body.

5 Take the third face cloth, tuck the lower point underneath, and press the fold flat using the palm of your hand.

6 Place the face cloth onto the top part of the ladybug shape, then tuck the three remaining points behind to form the head.

7 Now mold and shape the edges of the ladybug to make a smooth and softly rounded silhouette.

8 Add black felt circles for the spots and black and white circles for the eyes (see p. 77 for templates). To make the legs, fold and twist each pipe cleaner around itself.

54

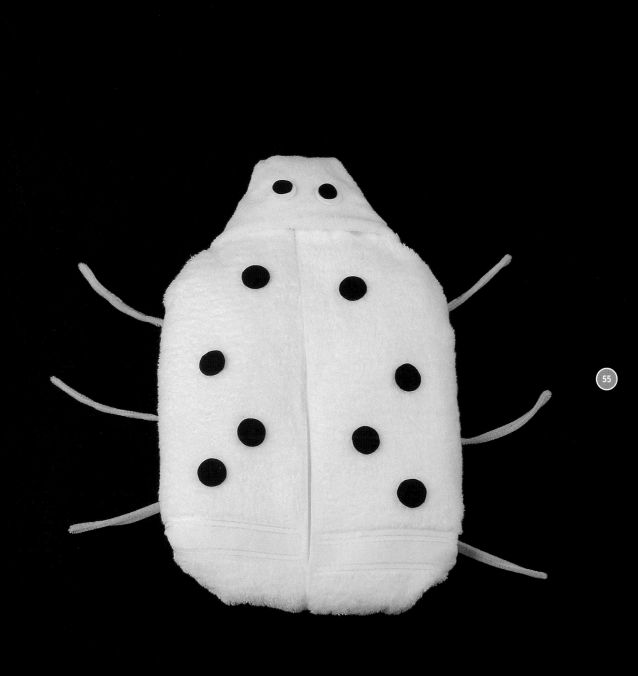

Angel Fish

Inspired by happy memories of sunny holidays in a tropical paradise, these little angel fish can be made from a single color or a combination of pastel or bright colors. As the shape is a simple one, it translates well for towels both large and small, and for face cloths, too. It's a simple task to create a whole shoal of little fishes to swim across the foot of the bed. Not quite the same as being in a tropical paradise, but still lots of fun!

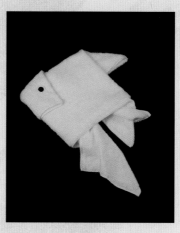

YOU WILL NEED

1 HAND TOWEL
2 FACE CLOTHS
BLACK AND WHITE FELT OR
1 CHOCOLATE

moderate

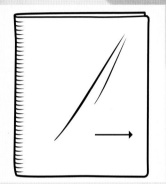  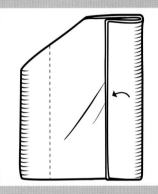

1 Lay the hand towel out horizontally, then fold in half widthways by bringing the left-hand edge over to meet the right. Press the fold flat using the palm of your hand.

2 Fold the top left-hand corner underneath the shape as shown, then press the fold flat. The diagonal edge should lie approximately at the halfway point along the top and left-hand edge.

3 Fold the shape in half widthways to indicate the center, then open out the shape again. Fold each side inward so they meet at the center crease line. Press the folds flat.

Square face cloths are excellent for making a little entourage of tiny fish to accompany a larger fishy fellow made from a bath towel.

TOP TIP

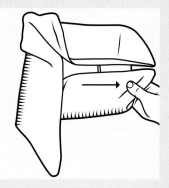

4 Divide the shape roughly into four again but horizontally this time, then fold the top and bottom edges toward the center and press the folds flat.

5 Pull out the left-hand point that lies inside the top fold. When the point is released from the fold, arrange it so it points downward, then press it flat.

6 Repeat with the other point that lies inside the fold on the right-hand side, but this time arrange it so that it points away from the shape. Repeat with the point that lies inside the upper fold as shown.

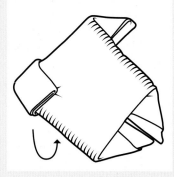

7 Slip one hand under the shape and lay the other flat on the top. Now flip the shape over to the other side, keeping all the folds in place. The previous points will now resemble fins.

8 Take two face cloths, grasp each one in the center, and run the cloth through your hands to form a fin shape. Add one to the tail and tuck the other under the head fold. Add a chocolate or felt eye.

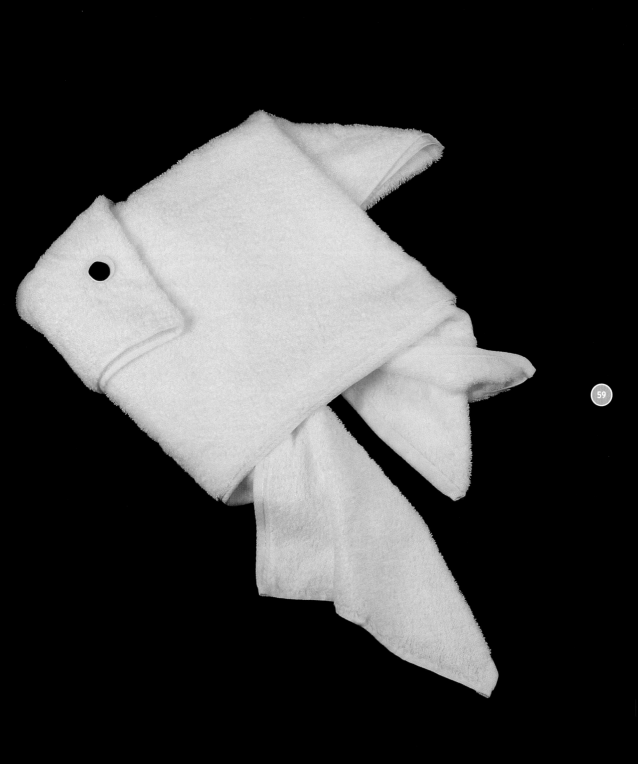

Cute Pooch

I challenge even the most steadfast non-dog-lover not to adore this irresistible little pooch! Anyone, especially children, will love to see this fellow greet them as they walk into their bedroom or bathroom. Based essentially on the elephant shape with a few slight variations, he's straightforward to make, and the quick addition of the felt features piles on the cheeky charm.

YOU WILL NEED	1 BATH SHEET 1 HAND TOWEL BLACK, WHITE, AND RED FELT 1 SAFETY PIN

moderate

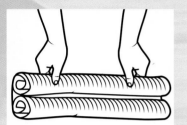  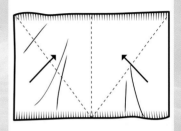

1 Lay the bath sheet out horizontally, fold in half to indicate the center, then open out again. Now roll both the long edges toward the center.

2 Take the rolled shape and bend it to form the dog's body, making sure that the rolls are facing outward. Tuck one end of the shape under so it resembles the back legs in a sitting position.

3 For the head, lay the hand towel out, fold in half widthways to indicate the center, then open out again. Now bring the two bottom corners to meet at the center of the top edge, then press the folds flat.

61

Fido doesn't have to sit up all the time. Simply flatten the rolled-up leg shape so he appears to be lying down, then balance the head on the shape as before.

TOP TIP

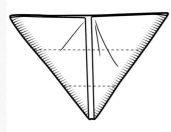

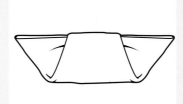

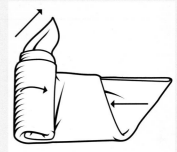

4 Fold the resulting triangle roughly into thirds horizontally as shown, press the folds flat to indicate the divisions, then open out the shape again.

5 Fold the lower point up to meet the second division line, then fold the lower edge to meet the top edge as shown. Press the folded shape flat using the palm of your hand.

6 Take the point at each side and roll up tightly to meet at the center, then pull out the two points a little. At this point secure the rolled shape using a safety pin.

7 Turn the shape over to the other side. Fold the points downward over the dog's face to form the ears. You can roll the edge that lies across the base of the points to release them a little more for shaping.

8 Balance the head on the body, apply a felt patch over one eye position, then add felt eyes, nose, and tongue to complete (see p. 76-77 for templates). Position the features so as to give your pooch the cutest expression!

Swimming Swan

Seven swans a-swimming? Well,
maybe just one or two would
be enough to make the point!
This classic towel origami model
demands to be created from the
largest, fluffiest, and most luxurious
of all the whitest towels you can
find! This elegant bird works perfectly
alone, or a pair can be used to great
effect when arranged symmetrically.

YOU WILL NEED

1 BATH SHEET
SUNGLASSES
2 FACE CLOTHS (OPTIONAL)
2 SAFETY PINS

difficult

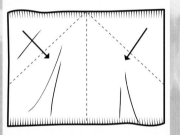

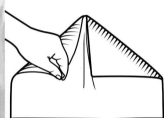

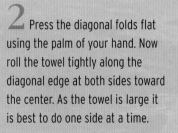

1 Lay out the bath sheet horizontally, then fold in half widthways to indicate the center and press the fold flat. Open up the towel again, then fold the top two corners down to meet at the center.

2 Press the diagonal folds flat using the palm of your hand. Now roll the towel tightly along the diagonal edge at both sides toward the center. As the towel is large it is best to do one side at a time.

3 When the first side is rolled up tightly, do the same on the other side so the shape is symmetrical. Make sure the first roll does not loosen as you complete the second.

Why not make a few cygnets from face cloths or small hand towels to complete the family group? You could also place some attractive fragrant soaps or bottles of bath product on the swan's back for your guest to enjoy at bath time.

TOP TIP

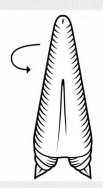

4 Now slip one hand underneath the rolled-up shape and place the other hand on top. Quickly flip the shape over to the other side. This is the swan body.

5 Place your hand on the swan's back and shape the rolled point to form the curved neck. You may have to use a little gentle force to make the neck stay in shape!

6 Locate the edge of the towel that lies across the rolled-up points at the back. Take the edge and roll it back on itself. This action will cause the points to splay outward.

7 Coax the points out a little more and arrange them to form the swan's wings. This will also help the stability of the shape. You can tuck a face flannel into each side to make the wings appear larger.

8 Add a pair of sunglasses to complete this elegant fowl. The weight of the sunglasses also helps to maintain the nicely curved shape of the neck. Use a couple of pins to keep the glasses in place.

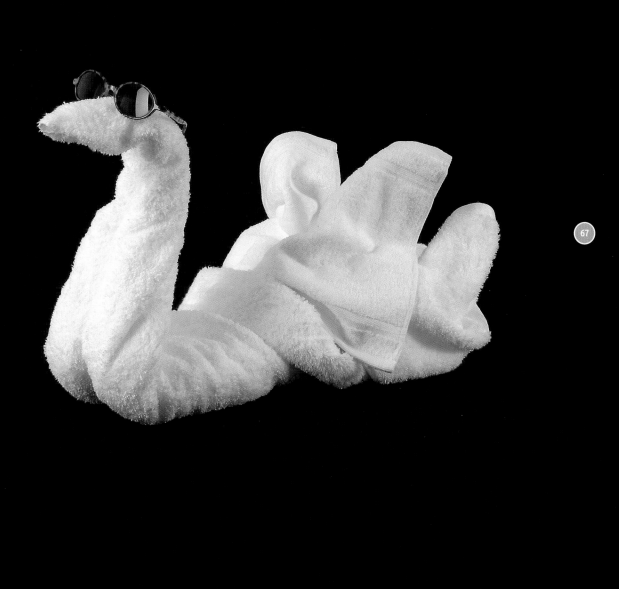

Monkey Business

This cheeky little guy can be arranged to sit on a bed or chair quite easily (although his head may need a little assistance from a safety pin). Use sunglasses to add character to his face or simply cut out some felt circles for eyes. The body shape holds together very well due to the nature of the rolls and twists, allowing a little more scope for creative expression. You can hang the monkey by one or both arms from the shower rail in the bathroom, but be sure to use another safety pin to secure his arm so that he stays put!

YOU WILL NEED	1 BATH SHEET 1 HAND TOWEL BLACK AND WHITE FELT OR 2 CHOCOLATES 3 SAFETY PINS

difficult

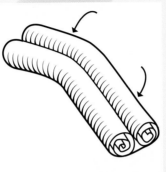

1 Lay the bath sheet out flat vertically, then fold in half lengthways and press the fold flat to indicate the center, then open out flat again. Roll both the short edges tightly toward the center.

2 Grasp the rolled-up bath sheet in both hands and bend it in the middle. Make sure that the rolls do not loosen as you do so and that the rolls face outward.

3 Find the corner of the bath sheet inside each roll and pull each one out a little. Take two corners in each hand, then pull out firmly in the direction of the arrows. This can be a little difficult at first.

If you choose to use pins instead of safety pins, make sure that they are large and have colored glass heads. This will ensure that they do not get lost in the fluffy pile of the towel.

TOP TIP

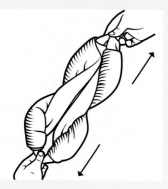

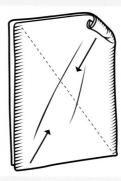

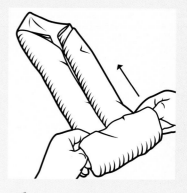

4 The rolls will tighten as you pull out the points, which in turn will twist to form the monkey's arms and legs. The area in the center can be manipulated to form the body.

5 For the head, lay the hand towel out flat then fold in half widthways. Press the fold flat. Now roll the towel diagonally from the top right and bottom left-hand corners toward the center.

6 Hold the rolls in one hand then roll the bottom point up toward the free points using the other hand. This will form a tight ball shape and the basis of the monkey's head.

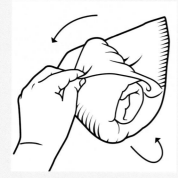

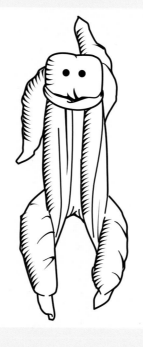

7 Turn the rolled shape over and peel the top layer of the point backward to cover the shape and to form the monkey's mouth. Tuck all the ends into the folds behind the head and secure using a safety pin.

8 Arrange the monkey's body so he can sit up or hang from the shower rail, then balance the head on top. Use a safety pin to secure the head to the body. Add black and white felt eyes (see template p. 77), or small round chocolates secured with double-sided tape.

Elephant Ahoy!

What a surprise your guests will have to find an elephant on their bed! For even more impact, try making a mini herd of jumbos, varying in size from a tiny one made from a face cloth and a small hand towel, to a real whopper using a bath sheet and a large bath towel! This model works well in plain white towels, but for a really authentic look use gray ones. Or, for an amusing twist on the theme, use pink.

YOU WILL NEED

1 BATH TOWEL
1 HAND TOWEL
BLACK AND WHITE FELT
OR 2 CHOCOLATES
1 SAFETY PIN

difficult

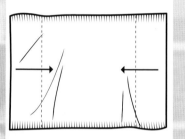

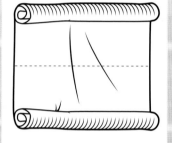

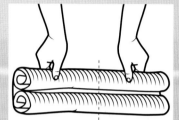

1 Lay the bath towel out flat horizontally, then fold along both short ends and press the folds flat. This will make the lower legs a little fatter so Jumbo can stand up by himself.

2 Now fold the towel in half lengthways. Press the fold flat to indicate the center and open out. Now roll the towel up tightly from both long edges so the rolls meet at the crease line in the center.

3 Grasp the rolled-up bath towel in both hands and bend it in the middle, keeping the rolled side facing outward. Try to make sure that the rolls do not loosen as you do this.

The rolled-up head and trunk shape can sometimes unroll itself. Secure the shape using a safety pin so that Jumbo won't lose his head while in situ on your guest's bed or in the bathroom!

TOP TIP

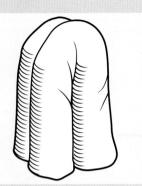

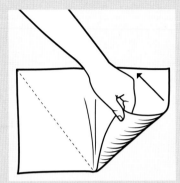

4 Stand the shape up and open out the rolls at the base of each "leg" if necessary so that Jumbo will stand sturdily on a flat surface. You have now completed the elephant body.

5 For the head, lay the hand towel out flat, fold in half widthways, and press the fold flat to indicate the center. Open the towel out again then bring both lower corners to meet the top edge at the center.

6 Roll both diagonal edges toward the center. It is best to do both sides at the same time, if possible. The point at the center will curl slightly, forming the trunk.

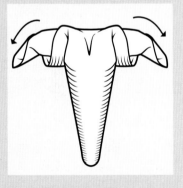

7 Turn the shape over and hold the trunk firmly in one hand, then pull down both upper points to form the ears. Open out the towel fabric a little to make a wider ear shape.

8 Place the head onto the body, then add a pair of eyes made from cut-out felt circles (see template p. 77), or chocolates secured with double-sided tape, or sunglasses!

Templates

Accessorize your fabulous foldings
with eyes, a nose, and other fun
additions in felt or construction
paper. Use these life-size templates
to create the features for the models
in this book.

Cute Pooch eyes

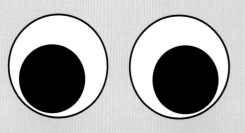

Cute Pooch nose

Cute Pooch tongue

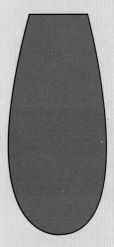

1 Trace these shapes onto sheets of tracing paper, then cut out and pin to colored felt.

2 Cut out the shapes and apply to your model, fixing firmly in place using glass-headed pins or tabs of double-sided adhesive tape.

Cute Pooch eyepatch

Eyes for all models

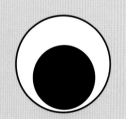

Ladybug spots

Skyscraper

1 For the skyscraper templates, trace each shape once onto a sheet of tracing paper.

2 Cut out each tracing paper shape and fix to the reverse side of silver-colored paper with removable adhesive tape.

3 Carefully cut out the required number of shapes from the silver paper, and apply to your model using tabs of double-sided adhesive tape.

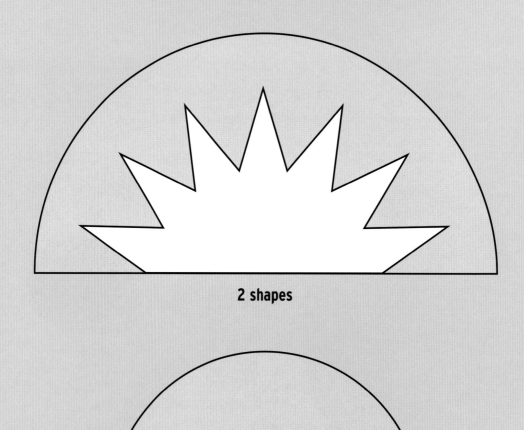

2 shapes

2 shapes

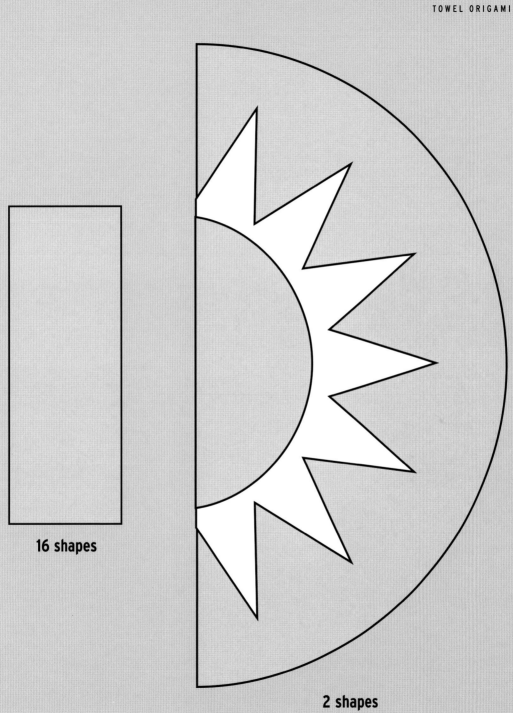

16 shapes

2 shapes

Index

Acknowledgments

The publishers are
grateful to Christy for
supplying the towels used
to make the projects in
this book.

www.christy-towels.com

Stockist number: 08457 585252